Step Into Magic: 21 Whimsical Poems For Curious Kids"

The Magical Shoes

ASHWANI

BookLeaf Publishing

India | USA | UK

Made with ❤ on the BookLeaf Publishing Platform
www.bookleafpub.in
www.bookleafpub.com

Dedication

To my beloved mother, Shakuntala,
Whose gentle hands guided my first steps,
And whose stories filled my world with magic.
For every bedtime tale, every warm hug,
And for teaching me to believe—
That imagination has wings,
And kindness is the greatest superpower.
This book is for you,
With all my love.

Preface

✧ Preface ✧

Step Into Magic: 21 Whimsical Poems for Curious Kids

Dear Reader — especially the curious, the dreamers, and the big-hearted little ones,

Welcome to a world where socks giggle, umbrellas fly, lunchboxes time-travel, and stars whisper their secrets to those who listen closely. This book was written with a simple wish: to keep the magic of childhood alive, one playful poem at a time.

Each poem in these pages is a tiny doorway—just big enough for your imagination to step through. Whether you're reading under the covers with a flashlight, curled up on a rainy afternoon, or sharing stories with someone you love, may these verses bring you joy, laughter, and a sense of wonder that never fades.

♥ **To all children:** You are the heartbeat of this book. Never stop asking "what if?", never stop imagining the impossible, and always believe that ordinary things can lead to extraordinary adventures.

♥ **To my wife:** Your love is the quiet magic behind every line. Thank you for being my guiding light, my calm, and my forever believer.

♥ **To our children and the child in all of us:** May these poems be a spark that lights up your dreams—and reminds you that magic is real... if only you believe.

With love and imagination,

Ashwani Devgune

Acknowledgements

🐞 Acknowledgments 🐞

Creating *Step Into Magic* has been a journey filled with wonder, late-night scribbles, cups of tea, and boundless imagination—and it wouldn't have been possible without the love and support of so many.

First and foremost, I offer my heartfelt thanks to **my wife**, whose unwavering support, quiet strength, and belief in my words gave this book its wings. You are the real magic behind the scenes.

To **my children**, and all the little dreamers who have inspired these poems—your laughter, questions, and sparkling eyes remind me every day why stories matter.

To the **teachers, parents, and bedtime readers**, thank you for passing on the magic of storytelling and poetry. The time you spend reading with children helps shape a more imaginative and compassionate world.

A warm thank you to **my friends and creative companions** who encouraged me to dream big, polish every rhyme, and believe in the magic of words.

To the illustrators, editors, and future readers—thank you for bringing life and light to these poems.

And finally, to **every curious kid** holding this book in their hands:

Keep dreaming, keep wondering, and remember—

the world is full of hidden magic, waiting just for you.

With deep gratitude,

1.  The Magical Shoes

I found a pair of shiny shoes,
Tucked beneath the bed,
With laces glowing rainbow-bright
And stars around the tread.
I slipped them on—just for some fun,
Not knowing what they'd do,
But then they **wiggled**, **buzzed**, and **whooshed**,
And off the ground I flew!
I soared above the cityscape,
Then zoomed across the sea,
I danced with dolphins in the waves,
And shared some cake and tea!
Through jungles deep and deserts wide,
They took me every place,
With every jump, I met a friend,
And wore a happy face.
But when the sun began to set,
The shoes said, "Time to go!"
They landed me back in my room,

With one last magic glow.
So if you find a pair like mine,
Don't rush or be afraid—
Just tie the laces, dream out loud,
And watch adventures made!

2.  The Talking Backpack

I found a pair of shiny shoes,
Tucked beneath the bed,
With laces glowing rainbow-bright
And stars around the tread.
I slipped them on—just for some fun,
Not knowing what they'd do,
But then they **wiggled**, **buzzed**, and **whooshed**,
And off the ground I flew!
I soared above the cityscape,
Then zoomed across the sea,
I danced with dolphins in the waves,
And shared some cake and tea!
Through jungles deep and deserts wide,
They took me every place,
With every jump, I met a friend,
And wore a happy face.
But when the sun began to set,
The shoes said, "Time to go!"

They landed me back in my room,
With one last magic glow.
So if you find a pair like mine,
Don't rush or be afraid—
Just tie the laces, dream out loud,
And watch adventures made!

3. 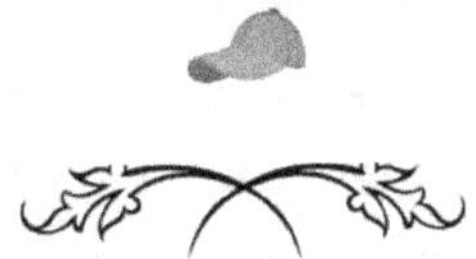 The Mischievous Hat

I found a hat upon a bench,
It didn't match—not mine, nor French.
It gave a wink, then spun around,
And floated gently off the ground!
I placed it right upon my head,
It whispered softly, "Fun ahead!"
Then off I ran with feet so fast,
Each step more thrilling than the last.
It made me sing in silly tones,
And dance atop the garden stones.
It turned my voice into a tune,
That made the flowers laugh till noon.
The squirrels all saluted me,
The birds began a jubilee!
And every time I struck a pose,
My nose would sparkle like a rose.
But just as I began to speak,

The hat leapt off and pinched my cheek.
"Adventure's done—for now, dear friend,
But magic starts where rules can bend."
Now every time I see a hat,
I smile and give a tip of that.
For you never know where it has been,
Or what wild things it's hiding in.

4.  The Umbrella That Followed Me Home

It wasn't raining, not one drop,
When I saw it leaning by the shop.
A purple umbrella, tall and wide,
With polka dots and stripes outside.
It wiggled once, then hopped in place,
I giggled at its friendly face.
It twirled around, then gave a spin—
"Mind if I come home with you? I hate the bin!"
I took it home and set it near,
But soon I heard it loud and clear:
"Let's not wait for stormy skies,
I've got tricks you won't believe your eyes!"
It opened up with a cheerful snap,
And pulled me in—just like a trap!
But soft inside, like cotton skies,
With jellybean clouds and firefly pies.
We floated high, then dipped down low,

We danced with penguins made of snow.
A gentle breeze, a swirling gleam—
It felt like stepping in a dream.
Then, POP! We landed safe and sound,
The umbrella folded with a bound.
It tipped itself like a fancy hat,
And whispered, "Tomorrow we'll chat."
Now every day it stays right there,
Beside the door and comfy chair.
And though the sky may still be blue,
It hides a secret world or two...

5.  The Blanket That Could Fly

At bedtime when the lights went low,
And stars began their gentle glow,
I pulled my blanket to my chin—
And that's when all the fun began!
It gave a twitch, then flapped a side,
And whispered, "Kid, let's take a ride!"
Before I blinked or counted sheep,
We zoomed beyond the world of sleep.
We soared through clouds of whipped cream swirl,
And looped around a moonbeam curl.
We played with stars in hide-and-seek,
And slid down Saturn's golden peak.
A comet waved as it passed by,
While dream whales danced across the sky.
We sipped hot cocoa with a bear
Who wore a bowtie in his lair.
The blanket wrapped me safe and tight,
And hummed a song of soft moonlight.

It said, "The world is big and wide,
But dreams can take you far inside."
And just before the morning sun,
It whooshed me back—our flight was done.
I woke up warm, with stars in mind,
And crumbs of cloud I'd left behind.
Now every night I smile and say,
"Let's take a trip the magic way!"
And as I dream, I softly lie—
Inside my blanket that can fly.

6. ✏ The Pencil That Drew by Itself ✏

I found a pencil, plain and gray,
It rolled beneath my desk one day.
No eraser, a little chipped—
But when I touched it, it gently flipped!
It sprang to life with scribbly cheer,
And whispered, "Let's make fun appear!"
It zoomed across my paper sheet,
With loops and lines that looked so neat.
It drew a castle, bold and grand,
With candy trees and jelly land.
A dragon smiled, a queen gave tea,
All sketched in swirls just perfectly.
Then came a ship with paper sails,
And mice in boots with tiny tails.
It scribbled stars, then clouds that flew—
Each picture shimmered as it grew.
I tried to write my name in ink,

But it was gone—gone in a blink!
The pencil tapped, "No need for fame,
Adventure's more than just a name."
And just before the final line,
It drew a frame with loops so fine—
Inside it said: "Let dreams run wild,
The world is yours, dear magic child."
Now in my drawer it sleeps each night,
But comes to life when thoughts take flight.
So if you find a pencil plain—
It might just sketch a candy train!

7.  The Tree That Told Stories

Behind my house, where daisies grow,
Stands a tree from long ago.
Its bark is cracked, its branches wide,
And tiny secrets live inside.
I sat beneath it, book in hand,
When suddenly it seemed… so grand!
A leaf fell gently on my page,
Then came a voice both wise and sage:
"Young dreamer there, with curious eyes,
Would you like tales beneath these skies?
I've seen the world from root to crown—
So settle in, I'll share them down."
It told of owls who ruled the night,
And squirrels who danced in silver light.
Of rabbits wearing capes of moss,
And ladybugs that flew across.

It spoke of winds that carried songs,
And rivers humming all day long.
It shared a tale of pirate bees,
Who hid their honey in the trees!
I listened close, my heart so still,
Each word a breeze, a gentle thrill.
Its voice like leaves in rustling rhyme—
A bedtime story out of time.
Now every day I visit there,
With grassy knees and wind-blown hair.
The tree just waits, so calm, so wise—
With branches full of soft surprise.

8.  The Cookie That Wanted a Friend

I reached into the cookie tin,
And heard a tiny voice within.
It wasn't loud, but oh, so clear—
"Excuse me... could you lend an ear?"
I peeked inside with curious eyes,
And found a cookie—quite a surprise!
It had two chips shaped like a grin,
And frosting freckles on its chin.
"I'm not just any treat, you see,"
It said while hopping up on me.
"I'm baked with joy, a pinch of fun,
And dreams that rise like morning sun!"
"I've waited here for quite a while,
For someone kind to share a smile.
I don't want crumbs or just one bite—
I want a friend to share delight!"
So off we went, that cookie and I,

We raced a bee, we chased a pie.
We built a fort of sugar cubes,
And sang with spoons in kitchen tubes!
But soon it sighed, "It's time to go—
A cookie's life is short, you know.
But thanks to you, I've had my day,
With laughter sweet in every way."
I gave it one small, gentle hug,
Then placed it back upon the rug.
And though it's gone, I know it's true—
The kindest friends are baked in *you*.

9.  The Xylophone That Sang the Weather

Tucked away in Granny's loft,
I found a treasure, dusty, soft.
A xylophone with colors bright—
Each key a shade of day or night.
I struck the red one—clang! A breeze!
Then blue—*a drizzle through the trees!*
The green one hummed a stormy beat,
And gold? It brought the desert heat!
The xylophone began to play
Its own wild tune of night and day.
A melody of thunder's roll,
With raindrops tapping on a bowl.
A snowflake danced with every note,
While clouds in rhythm seemed to float.
The sun peeked in with shining rays,
And tiptoed through the rainbow's maze.
I played a song, both fast and slow,
And watched the seasons come and go.

Spring chimed in with flower blooms,
While winter shook its frosty plumes.
But then it whispered, low and clear,
"Music shapes what we hold dear.
Strike your chords with joy and light—
And skies will always turn out right."
Now when I wish for sun or snow,
I climb the loft and start the show.
For in those keys, the skies are tethered...
To a xylophone that sings the weather.

10.  The Whispering Library Book 📖

In the quiet library's farthest nook,
I found a dusty, leather book.
Its cover glowed with faded gold,
Its pages curled, its edges old.
I reached to take it from the shelf,
And heard it whisper to itself.
"Another reader... kind and bright.
Come closer now—I'll share the light."
I opened wide to Chapter One,
And suddenly the words would run!
They danced around and formed a stream,
That pulled me into a waking dream.
A castle rose in candlelight,
A wizard soared in robes of white.
The trees could talk, the rivers sang,
And wolves wore rings with golden fangs.
Each page I turned revealed a door—

To lands I'd never seen before.
A pirate ship! A sky balloon!
A midnight race across the moon!
But just before I reached the end,
The book gave one last message penned:
"The stories live inside of you—
Be brave, be kind, and read things *new*."
I closed the book and heard it sigh,
Then slipped it back with a soft goodbye.
And now when silence starts to creep,
I know some books don't just *sleep*.

11.  The Giggling Socks

This morning as I dressed for school,
I found two socks—both soft and cool.
But when I slipped them on my feet,
They burst into a laughing beat!
"He tickles!" cried the one on right.
The left one giggled with delight.
"Hold on," I said, "this isn't fair!"
But both just wiggled in the air.
They danced and twirled upon the floor,
Then scooted sideways to the door.
"We're tired of hiding in the drawer—
Let's see what socks are really for!"
They marched me out without my shoes,
Across the lawn, beneath the dews.
We hopped on puddles, skipped through chalk,
And joined a ticklish toad for talk.
We tiptoed past a line of ants,
Then tangoed with some garden plants.

A cat meowed and tried to chase—
But socks just giggled, changed their pace!
At last they slowed, then whispered low,
"It's time to rest—no more to go."
They slid back on and hugged my toes,
Still soft and warm, like bedtime prose.
Now every time I feel a twitch,
Or hear a giggle in a glitch—
I know my socks are wide awake,
Just waiting for a chance to shake!

12. 🌙 The Pillow That Granted Dreams 🌙

My pillow looked like any kind—
So soft, so plain, so gently lined.
But one night when I turned to sleep,
It gave a puffy, dreamy beep.
"Hello," it said, "just close your eyes,
And I'll unveil some sweet surprise.
For every wish your heart holds tight,
I turn to dreams throughout the night."
So I wished to ride a comet tail,
And zoom through stars beyond the pale.
I wished to meet a talking fox,
Who taught me how to open locks.
I wished for wings—a dragon's pair,
To fly through jellybean-scented air.
I dined with giants, climbed the moon,
And danced in socks that sang a tune.
Each dream was stitched with magic thread,
That softly glowed beneath my head.

And when I woke at morning's light,
My pillow sighed, "Did dreams take flight?"
Now every night I whisper low,
Before I let the lamplight go:
"Dear pillow, take me where you please—
To candy clouds or laughing trees."
And sure enough, I float and gleam—
Upon the pillow that grants each dream.

13. ⊠ The Mirror with a Mind of Its Own ⊠

There's a mirror in my room,
Just plain and quiet, full of gloom.
But one odd day, it gave a blink—
Then smiled at me with eyes of ink!
"Hello there, friend," it softly said,
"I'm not just here to check your head.
I see beyond the socks you wear—
I see the magic in your stare."
I touched the glass—it rippled wide,
And pulled me through the other side!
A jungle bloomed with skies of pink,
And birds that sang in rhymes, not ink.
A lion wore a velvet vest,
A turtle ran (and beat the rest!).
A moonfish flew with candy fins,
And mountains laughed in rolling spins.
The mirror led me near and far,
Through castles made of cookie jar,

Past gumdrop trees and firefly lakes,
And dragons baking birthday cakes!
But soon it said, "Now back you go,
The real world needs your inner glow.
But don't forget what you have seen—
You're braver than you've ever been."
Now every day before I leave,
I glance once more and still believe.
That deep within, both wild and true,
Is magic waiting inside *you*.

14.  The Time-Traveling Lunchbox

I opened up my lunch one day,
And something strange flew out my tray—
A swirl of light, a spark, a pop!
Then time itself began to stop.
My sandwich gave a sudden cheer,
"My dear," it said, "You're not from here!
This lunchbox isn't quite your own—
It travels time! And not alone."
Before I spoke, it gave a spin,
And *whoosh!* the world came rushing in.
I blinked—and found myself with kings,
And knights who fought with feathered wings!
A juice box beeped and turned to gold,
While grapes turned into shields of old.
A robot lunch from future space
Said, "Pass the chips and join the race!"
I soared through ages, far and near,

Through dino days and Martian cheer.
Each bite became a ticket ride,
Through history's great, delicious tide.
But when the final bell had rung,
The lunchbox zipped, the portals flung.
It hummed, "Let's keep this just between
The bravest luncher ever seen."
Now every day I lift the lid,
And wonder where I'll go, well hid.
For even meals can hide surprise—
When lunchboxes are *time-wise*.

15.  The Flashlight That Showed the Invisible

I found it in a drawer so deep,
Beside old socks and buttons cheap.
A flashlight, small, with silver trim—
Its light was soft, its glow was dim.
But when I clicked it on at night,
It didn't shine just normal light.
It sparkled strange in purple gleam—
And showed me things you'd never dream!
My curtains danced a secret jig,
My slippers wore a powdered wig.
The wall had windows none could see,
That blinked and opened just for me.
A teacup waved from on the shelf,
The broom was sweeping by itself!
A ghostly cat with stripes of blue
Purred softly as it wandered through.
I gasped, I giggled, I explored,

Each flash revealed a world adored.
Invisible friends! A bubble band!
A tiny dragon on my hand!
Then came a whisper near my ear:
"You see the things we all hold dear.
Magic hides in every place—
Just shine your light and find its face."
Now every night, I scan my room,
And watch the shadows shift and bloom.
With flashlight close and wonder wide,
I see the world that lives... inside.

16.  The Scarf That Controlled the Wind

I found a scarf both long and bright,
With colors bold like morning light.
It shimmered soft in sky-blue thread,
And wrapped itself around my head.
It whispered, "Child, don't you know?
I'm not just made for winter snow.
With just a tug, a twist, a spin—
You'll feel the dance of wild wind in!"
I twirled it once—*a gentle breeze!*
It rustled through the apple trees.
I looped it twice—a stronger blow,
That made the windmills whirl and go!
Then three times 'round—oh, what a flight!
Leaves soared like birds in sweet delight.
The kites flew high with cheerful squeal,
And hats took off behind a wheel!
The clouds obeyed my scarf's command,
They drifted slowly over land.

I cleared the sky for sunshine's play,
Then swirled a breeze to end the day.
But when I tried a mighty spin,
The scarf grew still, then tucked me in.
"Power is fun," it said with grace,
"But only when used in the right place."
Now when the wind begins to hum,
I smile, knowing what may come.
For wrapped around my neck so kind,
Is the scarf that plays with *wind and mind.*

17. ☒ The Helmet That Heard the Stars ☒

In Grandpa's shed, all full of dust,
I found a helmet, edged with rust.
It looked like one from outer space,
With buttons, beeps, and cosmic grace.
I placed it gently on my head—
And suddenly, the stars all *said*:
"Welcome, child with heart so wide.
We've waited long to be your guide."
I heard them sing in twinkling tones,
In lullabies and comet moans.
The moon hummed deep, a silver song,
While planets clapped and chimed along.
One star said, "We were born from light,
We danced through day, we blinked through night.
We watched your Earth grow kind and green,
And held your dreams we've always seen."
I asked them things I'd never told—
About being small, about being bold.

They sparkled back with soothing sound,
"There's stardust in you—look around."
Each night since then, I sit so still,
And wear that helmet on the hill.
The stars still sing, both near and far—
Their voices shaped in who you are.
So if you hear a nighttime breeze,
That whispers through the tallest trees—
It might just be a star you knew,
Sending a glowing song to *you*.

18.  The Paintbrush That Brought Things to Life

I found a paintbrush in a case,
Tucked quietly inside my base.
Its handle shimmered blue and red,
With tiny stars around the head.
I dipped it in my old paint tray,
Just messing 'round one rainy day.
I drew a cat with stripes of green—
And then it *stretched* and gave a lean!
It blinked at me and gave a purr,
Then brushed against me, soft as fur.
I gasped, then grinned from ear to ear—
This paintbrush made my *drawings* appear!
I painted fish that swam mid-air,
A jellybean tree, a flying chair.
A castle made of clouds and cream,
And boots that bounced like in a dream.
Each stroke became a living thing—

A bell, a bird, a crown, a king!
But then the brush began to slow,
Its spark grew faint, its glow let go.
It whispered, "Paint with heart, not speed—
Create with wonder, not with greed.
One thoughtful line can build a land,
Where kindness walks with colors grand."
Now when I paint, I pause and see
What kind of magic flows from me.
For with that brush, I've come to know—
Imagination makes life *glow*.

19.  The Clock That Could Pause Time

It sat upon my window shelf,
A tiny clock all by itself.
Its hands moved slow, its ticking light,
It blinked at me one quiet night.
It whispered, "Tick, then tock, then stop—
You hold the key to make time *drop*.
Just tap me thrice and hold your breath,
And I'll freeze time like whispered death."
I tried it once—tap, tap, tap—
The world went silent with a snap!
No breeze, no buzz, no dogs, no cars—
Just me beneath the frozen stars.
I watched a raindrop hang midair,
A paper plane just float and stare.
A squirrel froze mid-nutty chew,
While time stood still like sticky glue.
I raced around, I read ten books,
I drew on walls in secret nooks.

I made a fort from pillows tall,
And built a train with socks and all!
But when I felt the moment pass,
I tapped once more—like breaking glass.
The world resumed its spinning cheer,
As if I'd never disappeared.
Now every time I need a break,
To pause the rush, the noise, the ache—
I look up at that tiny chime...
And thank the clock that bends back time.

20. New Poem

21. New Poem

22.  The Candy That Spoke Animal

It looked like just a jellybean,
All speckled blue with limey green.
I found it in a candy tin,
And popped it in with a playful grin.
But oh! The moment that I chewed,
The world around me changed its mood.
A buzzing sound came loud and clear—
"Hey, human kid! Can you hear?"
I turned to find a squirrel near,
Tapping nuts with joy and cheer.
He grinned and said, "We've lots to say,
We've waited for this very day!"
The robins chirped, "At last, hooray!"
The turtles shared their jokes and play.
The ants formed lines and sang in parts,
While dolphins beamed with fishy hearts.
The dogs explained their tail-wag code,
The cats spoke poetry they wrote in ode.

A goldfish asked, "What's it like on land?"
While parrots danced and made demands!
I laughed and listened, shared my name,
And felt a part of nature's game.
That tiny bean—a gift so sweet—
Had bridged the world beneath my feet.
But soon its magic wore away,
Their voices dimmed by end of day.
The squirrel winked, "You'll always know—
We're here, just quiet, with tales to show."
Now when I walk beneath a tree,
I nod at birds and bumblebees.
For deep inside, I understand—
A candy helped me hear the land.

23. The Key Without a Door

I found a key beneath a tree,
It shimmered gold and smiled at me.
No lock, no door, no chest, no gate—
Just whispered softly, "You hold fate."
It didn't fit my closet lock,
Nor treasure chests, nor garden rock.
It hummed when held in morning sun,
As if some secret had begun.
I asked it, "Where's your home, dear key?"
It sparkled, "Only time will see.
I'm not for locks you twist and turn—
I'm for the *things* you're yet to learn."
I placed it in a velvet pouch,
Beside a feather, next to a couch.
Some days it glows, some days it's still—
Like it's waiting for a dream to fill.
Perhaps one day a map will show

Where keys like this are meant to go.
Or maybe, just beyond the wall,
There's something grand that waits us all.
So if you find a key like mine,
Don't rush—just wait, it's by design.
For magic lives in quiet things...
And keys can open *everything*.

♨ **To Be Continued...**
Watch the skies, listen at night,
The next adventure is taking flight...
Because magic never truly ends—
It only waits around the bends.